MW01488292

Something To Think About,
Something To Consider

Something To Think About, Something To Consider

§

Joseph B. Stingley

Copyright © 2015 Joseph B. Stingley
All rights reserved.

ISBN-13: 9781517701109
ISBN-10: 1517701104

Preface

My FIRST ENCOUNTER WITH GOD was when I had my first "remembrance" of seeing my guardian angel at the age of five. My older brother and I shared the same room growing up.

That particular night when we were told by our parents to turn the lights off and go to sleep, I wasn't sleepy. I proceeded to play with toy action figures in my bed in the dark. For some reason my spirit told me to turn the lights on for a moment.

When I did, I got a brief glance of my guardian angel sitting on our dresser drawer watching over us. After blinking my eyes to look again, the angel was gone. From that moment I became aware of my connection to God and the things of the Spirit, including the spirit world.

Through the years, I became keenly aware of God, studying about Him, becoming a follower of Christ Jesus, and learning the operations of the Holy Spirit (the Spirit). I am constantly aware that I need all three entities in my life.

Funny but more interesting is that as I have gotten older (spiritually), my sons Jeffrey Paul and Joseph David have cheered me on in my faith in God. One of the things I enjoy about them both is that they would allow me to lecture, speak, and teach them on a daily basis if I so desired.

I was born with a desire and natural gift and skill with great ability to teach, to communicate, to train, to impart. God has given things to me in various areas of my life that are more than just dissemination of information.

God has called me to a place of impartation. In other words, rather than just getting up and giving the lecture, the speech, or the talk, I gave the students the information. But something else comes out of me that is given by the Spirit of God.

And riding on the information is an impartation of the life of that word so that it goes inside them like a seed, and it produces something in their hearts. And God has allowed me to see...to see in their eyes that little light. And so I say, "Ah, they got it. They got it."

Not only do they get it, but it becomes life changing for them. This is where God stretches me and is stretching me right now. I'm not just a disseminator of information but one who gives out truth with impartation.

January 1

Our kindness and unconditional love will draw people to us, no matter how deep in darkness they are. When they come to us, we must not push them away like so many others have in the past. With the time I have left on this earth, I'm committed to being conformed and transformed into the image of God, and I know that all will experience His blessings when they come into my presence.

January 2

This year will be your best year yet! Pack your bags. Set your expectation for this new chapter to begin in your life. Expect new levels of life: spiritually, mentally, and physically. There is a divine and holy calling for you this year. Enter it with reverence and honor. Now is your time!

January 3

You control your way of thinking. Your mind doesn't care if you allow negative or positive thoughts to enter. Your mind will process and work with either one. The harvest of those thoughts will come forth. It will either be negative thoughts, which will lead you toward darkness, or it will be positive thoughts, which will lead you toward light.

January 4

Attitude is one of the most important words in our vocabulary. It determines how people act toward us and how we react toward them. God has blessed us with the ability to change our environment by changing our mind and thought patterns, which in turn will change our attitudes.

January 5

Today, if you haven't already, tell God how grateful you are for your life! Remind yourself that no matter what your situations are, it could be a whole lot worse. You are not dead yet!

January 6

As you settle down for the evening, I have a strong sense, a knowing, and a belief that God is working on your behalf, removing obstacles that have held you back for such a long time. I encourage you to expect divine appointments, divine opportunities, and divine solutions to appear in your life.

January 7

"Something great is happening to me right now!" I generally repeat this statement a few hundred times a day. I actually recorded the phrase and play it on repeat while I'm driving in my car. You could do the same! The more you repeat this statement, the more you will believe it, and the sooner you will start experiencing it in all areas of your life.

January 8

This year, move and grow into the consciousness of discovering just how powerful you can become when you look to God as the extension of all your strength. Depend on His wisdom, His direction,

His truth. Only then will you have conviction and confidence in yourself. You will remove the fears that held you back in the past. Let this new year be the year of God's truest potential in your life.

JANUARY 9

If you had life challenges this week, and even argued with God about them...make a decision today to give and release it all to God. Let Him handle it. You did in the past. He is yet in the business of taking care of His children: YOU!

JANUARY 10

Take time this weekend to reevaluate and maybe reprioritize the goals you set back in January of this year. Take time to refocus and to make sure you are still on course and moving forward at a steady pace.

JANUARY 11

Today, many of you are in need of wisdom regarding situations in your life. Whatever the situation is, God has the answer. The only requirement? Ask Him.

JANUARY 12

Old memories will try to come back to your mind telling you what a failure you are. These memories will also bring many other negative thoughts to your mind. You MUST tell the old memories out loud that they cannot come back, not even for a moment. The space they want to hang out in has been taken up by success. God has set you free from past failures and mistakes a long time ago. Tell those old memories you are free, free indeed.

JANUARY 13
Do you know that you have the ability to have a hugely positive impact on hundreds, even thousands of lives in your lifetime? My prayer for you this week is that you will seize the opportunities to be a positive leader, helping individuals progress in their lives on a daily basis. The endeavors may seem small, but inevitably they become big.

JANUARY 14
I really want you to consider this TONIGHT...if you find yourself angry with others, yourself, even God, get it right if at all possible before you go to sleep.

JANUARY 15
As you move about on this day, settle this in your mind and speak it with your mouth..."I am BLESSED. I am every good thing God declares me to be, and I am grateful for it all. Amen!"

JANUARY 16
Today, my prayer for you is "You will go through your day with your ears open to hear and your eyes open to see what God desires to say and do. I pray that you will release the great treasure you have inside you, as you hear and see how God wants you to share it with the world."

JANUARY 17

As you settle down for the evening, I want to tell you that God knows you completely! He has not forgotten your acts of love, in showing His love and serving others: in your job, in the yoga classes you teach, in your home, etc. These are not small things in God's eyes. Because of your faith in these things, you are creating a foundation of greater things to accomplish in the future.

JANUARY 18

Many times and more often than not, we study how darkness works, how it infiltrates our minds, our families, our jobs, even our spiritual walk. From personal experience, this route is not the one to pursue or spend time on. When we spend quality time in the presence of God, experiencing His favor, grace, mercy, and wisdom, we don't have to know how darkness and negativity comes about and its inner workings. Why? Because we have studied the light, spent quality time basking in the love of God, experiencing peace that surpassed natural understanding. We no longer know of God, we KNOW HIM. This is our success!

JANUARY 19

One of our greatest desires should be as we come into the presence of others, they will realize that we have been with God and He lives on inside of us. How can this be? It's pretty simple...you cannot spend quality time in the presence of God without all the things He is and not have them come upon you, such as His love, peace, compassion, strength, and brightness.

January 20

Today, be so interested in those you come in contact with that you will listen to the whispers of God; then follow through with what you heard. That whisper might tell you to buy someone's lunch, say an encouraging word, give a hug, or give an attentive ear. God is interested in every area of our lives: all of us. If we love God, we are also interested in what He is interested in!

January 21

This weekend, let us all slow down (including me). Let's only see the few feet in front of us. Don't be concerned about what's ahead. Just know there is a light in your path that is guiding you in all things. Your heart will tell you what's your next step. Again, slow down. Your answers are coming.

January 22

In 1973, there was a hunger in me to know who God was. So I dug in and looked at lots of data. God came into the midst of my research. In the end, I could not argue with the data: GOD IS REAL! I have a great heart for God, and I desire the same for you!

January 23

My prayer for you today…"I pray and speak God's blessings over you and invite you to accept that you are already a success in the eyes of God. I pray you seek the wisdom of God, regarding your unique gifts, skills, and talents, on how to bring healing to the world. Amen."

JANUARY 24

I am more expectant right now than I have ever been before! In the very near future, I see people receiving miracles they need from God. You, reading this post, set your expectations NOW for your miracle!

JANUARY 25

Our prayers, united together, being focus on awakening to God, will solve every crisis, every problem in our nation and our world. God is calling us to pray, and pray again!

JANUARY 26

No matter what darkness tries to tell you, refuse to let go of God's hand!

JANUARY 27

Over the past several years I learned something very powerful. The thoughts I have in my mind come to life when I speak them. The same applies to you. If we are not satisfied with what is happening in our lives, then we should try asking God to help change and correct our thoughts, our beliefs. With God's help, we can create a new world for ourselves, new beliefs, even a new life.

JANUARY 28

If you want to live a powerful life filled with victories, it will not happen without daily time set aside for fellowship with God. It's a goal that we have to pursue at all costs without fail. Daily fellowship with God is what will open up a life of supernatural power and consistency.

JANUARY 29

My meditation for the past several days has been: "I have the wisdom of God." However, this morning, I added the statement "God, You are real." It was like I was telling God…"I know for a fact: He is real in my life and my soul!" I felt I was meant to share this with you.

JANUARY 30

This Monday morning I pray that you reading this will see God as your Source, your Provision, and your Protection. I pray you take and leave all your care with Him and that you refuse to worry. Instead, you will pray, use your faith on purpose, believing God will bring you through all your problems without fail. Know that God is with you! Amen!

JANUARY 31

If people notice you have lost your foundation of peace, they will know you have not been steadfast in your quiet time with God. It's very important you prevail in the presence of God daily.

February 1

You are already a success if you have goals that are lined up with God's purpose for your life, and you are pursuing them with your total being. Very soon they will manifest themselves in your life.

February 2

Today, I'm grateful and thankful to see another day that I have never seen before nor will see again. I'm going to enjoy this day and rejoice in it.

February 3

This year, I'm grateful and thankful I get to experience another birthday. Some years ago I heard a whisper from God saying He would give me 120 years to live on this earth if I wanted to stay here that long. I have many years left. My goal for the remainder of my years is to reach out and help everyone to experience God's unconditional love through me, including the teaching of yoga, either with or without words. It is the Anointing, the Spirit of God that changes us inside and out.

February 4

I wanted to share one of my daily prayers with you today. This prayer just might speak to your heart. "Father, today I open my heart and mind to the great things You have in store for my future. I choose to be faithful. I choose to prepare. I won't look to the left or to the right, but I will keep my eyes on You!"

February 5

As you allow the light to shine in your life, that same light in you can lead others through the midnight challenges they are experiencing in their lives.

February 6

These written words are for someone this very moment...the faith in your heart and the words of your mouth will allow God to create a miracle for you!

February 7

As you settle down for the night, think about this: the more we grow up in love, the less we will allow different opinions of others tear us apart.

February 8

Today, make a decision to walk in the love of God toward others no matter what! Treat others with the love of God and not your own love. Why? Your love has limits, but God's love does not. Be a blessing to others. See what happens, and mainly see what happens to you on the inside.

February 9

A meditation for tonight: "God loves me just as I am."

FEBRUARY 10

The strongest person, man or woman in the physical world will never defeat darkness in the spiritual world. This battle will only be won in the spiritual realm. We are spiritual beings, we have a soul, we live in a body. If you have been wrestling with darkness in the physical world, change your tactics and take your fight to the spiritual realm. Your victory is there.

FEBRUARY 11

Today has been a great day! Before you go to bed tonight, make a decision to wake up tomorrow expecting great things to happen in your life.

FEBRUARY 12

Today my prayer is over your love ones and everyone to received the healing power of God, whether emotional or physical, I pray and speak healing from the top of their head to the soles of their feet, including both inside and out.

FEBRUARY 13

Today, I will only expect great things to happen in my life. I will keep my mind and thoughts positive, full of expectation, full of hope, and full of joy of all the good and great things God has in store for me. What about you?

FEBRUARY 14

I encourage you to not spend another second trying to be like someone else. This weekend, make a decision to be the COMPLETE you. Multitudes of people need YOU, just as you are.

FEBRUARY 15

I want to encourage you to keep making adjustments in your life, keep learning new things, including learning from past choices, keep asking for divine wisdom in solving the challenges you face. From personal experience, if you don't quit, you will wake up one day, no longer having to say in faith "All is well." You will be saying, "All is well," because it has NOW been manifested in your life.

FEBRUARY 16

I encourage you to use your faith on purpose for others. I'm sure you can think of at least three individuals who could use your faith in things they are believing in God for. Take this as a meditation and prayer as you ready yourself for bed tonight.

FEBRUARY 17

Today is already a success for you and me. We are alive. We have movement in our bodies and our minds are clear, strong, and fixed on the goodness of God.

FEBRUARY 18

If you have just one of these four things: family, friends, good health and not wanting for anything in your life, you are BLESSED. This evening as you settle down, don't forget to be grateful and give thanks for these because they are precious gifts!

FEBRUARY 19

You can become so strong in faith and in the love of God that you care so much about people, risking their rejection when you tell how much God loves them!

FEBRUARY 20

Every day you should take inventory on what's going on inside your soul. Look inside to see if you are at peace, maybe holding on to offenses, not trusting people anymore, among other things. At the end of it all, if what you find in your inventory doesn't agree with God's standards, immediately see that God is helping you to change. God is too good of a God and Father to keep anything in your heart that is not pleasing to Him.

FEBRUARY 21

Love does not run and hide. Love only reaches out. Love inspires us to become all things to all people. Take their hand. Love them just as they are.

February 22
As you move about your day, expect God to reveal things from His heart to yours. He wants you to know His will for your life.

February 23
Today, let us be "moved with compassion" to everyone that we meet. If you truly love God, you love people unconditionally!

February 24
Try this. Love people right where they are in their life. Love them unconditionally. Give them your support even if they are in a different place than you are in their lives. Ask God for wisdom in dealing with them. You will encourage and motivate them just by loving them right where they are. I'm speaking from experience. This is how we will change the world and make it a better place to live in.

February 25
Whatever your vision in life is, no matter how big you think or want it to be, God's vision for your life is much, much, much BIGGER than that! Don't resist the BIG vision God has for your life!

February 26
Today, you may have thought about giving up, either spirituality, emotionally, or physically. But you didn't. You persevered through today. Maybe before you go to sleep tonight, you can encourage

someone by e-mail, voice mail, text or in person, telling him or her to stay the course, as something great will happen to them tomorrow!

FEBRUARY 27

Your dreams and your goals are not impossible for you to achieve and surpass. You do need help in accomplishing them. You may not know who to talk to, who to contact, nor have the education, knowledge, skills, or finances to start. That is OK! Commit to pursuing dreams and goals, including writing a list of them. Then, spend time being still, meditating on divine appointments, divine connections, and divine relationships. It will not be long before what you see in the spirit world manifests itself in the physical world!

FEBRUARY 28

You may face challenges on a daily basis and sometimes several times a day. If you keep and maintain the right attitude (that is, a positive attitude), the challenges you encounter will not be as bad as you thought. Meditation will not only help you in this area of your life but will also bring about a consistency that others will begin to notice in you!

MARCH 1
Today was a good day! As you settle down for the evening, know that so many people believe in you, love you dearly, and will do whatever it takes to help you become successful!

MARCH 2
Make sure to pursue the vision that has been placed in your heart. You will be faced with many distractions. They could very well be divinely inspired, but they are for someone else to pursue.

MARCH 3
The mind must be controlled, disciplined, and made to conform even if it wants to do otherwise. It must be told what to do and made to conform. The process is challenging, but the blessings are everlasting. Meditation is a key factor in this process.

MARCH 4
Tell God all your needs. Then, thank Him for all He has done in your life!

MARCH 5
Next weekend you will have opportunities to share the goodness of God in your life. Don't be ashamed to share what God has done for and in your life. Let your light and testimony shine so that it will encourage and set them free from the darkness that has

invaded and taken residence in their mind. This weekend you will have the opportunity to touch, change and even help transform another person's life!

MARCH 6

Step out of your comfort zone and love people on purpose. If you come across people who are not so nice, maybe just downright rude, see them through the eyes of DIVINE LOVE. Look at them with a pureness of heart, being as polite as possible, showing them the divine love that lives on the inside of you. As you do this, loving people on purpose will become a habit, and you will become good at it.

MARCH 7

Is there a person who has influenced you in the past with their unconditional love and compassion toward you? And are you grateful that they did? Have you taken the time to express to them your thankfulness? If you have not, what is preventing you from taking a few minutes to express your appreciation today?

MARCH 8

I want to challenge you to pursue love. If you want to walk in the power of God, then pursuing love is the best way to develop this lifestyle and the best way for others to see God through you. Think about the healing and liberation of those who are oppressed with this POWER OF LOVE flowing in your life!

March 9
Today, I pray for everyone I know and don't know. I pray especially for our local, state, and national government leaders to guide and lead us with the wisdom of God, so we can live a quiet and simple life, in humble thoughtfulness. Amen. America is not going to pieces. America is not going to ruin. America is still the country that can and will bless the world. This is my belief.

March 10
Start your day by setting aside your own agenda and seek the wisdom of God instead. This is really the only permanent option in solving the problems you are confronted with.

March 11
Tonight, my meditation will be on God who brings transformation, who welcomes transformation, who commands transformation, and who is sovereign over transformation.

March 12
Today, it is the grace of God that has allowed me to live another day! This is not a gift that I can give to myself. This comes only from God, and I'm thankful for this reality. I have another day and opportunity to love and serve others!

MARCH 13

YOU CAN START TODAY...make the decision to come out of every damaging area of your life that has confined you for long enough. Once you make that decision, God will give you the power to carry it out!

MARCH 14

If we would take the time to ask God to put in us a sensitive spirit, we will become aware of so many people around us who need encouragement just as much as we do. It's time out for us being led by our physical eyes only. We need to be led by the Spirit. Just because we see people smiling doesn't mean they are happy.

MARCH 15

DON'T ANTICIPATE FEAR! Whatever you have been called you to do, you can do it. You will have the resources, the protection, and the provision to accomplish it.

MARCH 16

Most of us are active in some type of fitness or yoga training, and it is crucial that we continue in order to maintain our physical body. Spending time with God is a spiritual practice that we all should diligently become disciplined in also. The more you practice it, the easier it becomes. And, it is likely you will not achieve perfection in your spiritual training at first. You might fall flat and stumble. Don't stay there, get up and go at it again. Eventually, you will become fit and stronger in the things of God.

March 17

If anything is needed in your life at this very moment and you are unable to find a solution, consider God's grace. His grace will always make sure you have sufficiency in all things: an overflow of abundance.

March 18

Today was a good day! It's God's grace that empowers us to move forward.

March 19

As we move more into watching the words that come out of our mouths, we take responsibility of the thoughts in our mind when we accept those thoughts as ours and when we say them out loud. One way to fight the negative thoughts is that when they appear in your mind, your first response should be, "I don't receive that!" You might have to say this three hundred times a day. The negative thoughts will become fewer and will eventually cease.

March 20

If you are weak in your own eyesight (thoughts), eventually this is how others will see you. When the negative thoughts try and convince you that you will never be successful, refuse to believe and receive those thoughts. Dare to believe what God says you are. You are strong, courageous, successful, prosperous and well able to overcome every obstacle before you.

March 21

God will not send disasters in your life to destroy you because of your past, and current choices that are not lined up with His plan for your life. Instead, He will give you spiritual instructions to inspire you with love to seek His way of living that will bring prosperity to your spirit, soul, and body. If you hear, listen, accept, and move forward with His instructions, you will come forth stronger, powerful, and a mighty witness for His unfailing love.

March 22

As you are settling down for the night, I want to encourage you to stay open, don't limit yourself, and believe that your breakthrough is a possibility!

March 23

There is a world of people who need you just like I need you.

March 24

Keep spending time in God's presence. Believe His Word. Obey His instructions and refuse to quit until you can say, "All God's promises are now present in my life."

March 25

I want to encourage you to resist, don't feed, and don't consider anything darkness and negativity speaks or offers to you. Instead, become steadfast right where you are in life, until you receive all the things God has promised for you!

March 26

I'm praying for you today. God lives in the mist of your total being: your heart. Today, take the opportunity to let others know God lives in them, too. Your influence can be such a light they need at this time in their lives.

March 27

As we give to and receive from our brothers and sisters, as compassionate human beings, in spiritual and temporal ways, we are actually following God's teachings on "a journey of love." We should never miss opportunities to do good for others.

March 28

AS YOU START YOUR DAY...remember you don't need a history of successes behind you to answer your calling in life. You have great grace upon your life!

March 29

No matter how the economy is doing (good or not so good), your education (or lack of it) or your circumstances (great or not so great), there are so many people out there that need your words of encouragement, your testimonies of success in spite of severe challenges, and your great compassion to see them break away from all that has held them back! They are looking for people just like you!

MARCH 30

The reason so many find themselves struggling to accept God into their lives is because they get caught up with thoughts that God will not forgive them for the things they have done. They keep a repeating record (thoughts) of all the bad things they did. Those thoughts will keep you in a place of suffering and will have you believe that God's forgiveness is impossible, but it's not! All you have to do is to ask God to forgive you. As you ask with your mouth, believing in your heart: it's done! Now, let God fix all the things in your life that need fixing. Trust Him for and in all things. As you do, your heart will become open to His amazing love for you!

MARCH 31

Make time to slow down...find the SUNSHINE. The nicer the view, the better the thinking.

April 1

I truly believe when we learn to rest in confidence of the living God, peace will possess this world and it will be like heaven on Earth.

April 2

THIS VERY MOMENT...if you are frustrated and irritated, then you are not trusting God to take care of whatever you are challenged with! Give back to Him NOW!

April 3

As you start your day here is something to think about...what you center your thoughts and actions on you will get proficient at. If you are spending your day in never-ending battles, along with the stress it's creating for you, this means it is keeping you from your passion and your happiness. Today, make a conscious decision to take your life back!

April 4

We have complete control over how we respond to every situation that we might ever experience. This means it is our responsibility to think, evaluate, and reply in every situation according to God's love!

April 5

My prayer for you today..."That great grace will be upon you and that you will complete the job God has called you to do." I love you and pray favor over you every day!

April 6

MEDITATION FOR TONIGHT..."I receive peace of mind, wholeness, prosperity and health in every cell, every organ, every function of my body, and for every area of my life!" Now you walk in that meditation!

April 7

What you allow to take root inside your HEART grows ALWAYS. Doubt, unbelief, and fear will grow and keep you bound. Truth and faith will grow and make you free.

April 8

Your life is not your own. Every decision you make will not only affect you but others, too. And those others will make decisions that affect others, etc. Become aware and conscious of things you say, how you act and respond, including your body movements and facial expression. Let them all be done out of LOVE!

April 9

When you lay aside your life, you live to please God instead of yourself. You let your life be guided by His love. If love leads you to the person down your street, or across the hall on your job, you follow. When love calls you to pray for someone in need, you do just that. Commit yourself today to lay aside your own life and take up the life of love.

APRIL 10
My desire and prayer for you is "To Be Courageous!" You might be facing some challenging ordeals. But my desire and prayer for you is "Fear Not!" No matter what you are going through, my message to you is "Take Heart, Don't Be Afraid!"

APRIL 11
REMEMBER THIS...God knows what is ahead for you. He will shine just enough light for you to take one step at a time. You will have to continue walking in that light in order to get where you are going. I know for a fact that God will see to it that you have victory as you continue walking in the light.

APRIL 12
The moment you start thanking God for all that is going right in your life, you are on your way out of the problem. Just something to consider this evening.

APRIL 13
Tomorrow, step outside your everyday routine and position yourself in an atmosphere of faith, where hearing from God is easy and you can be a blessing to others. So many people are waiting just to experience you!

APRIL 14
When you find doing things the world's way, in the secular or natural realm, and it's not working, including the meditation,

spiritual, retreats, etc., there is another option that is the best option I have experienced: and that is going back to the basics, being in the presence of God, reading and studying His Word, believing and trusting Him in all things concerning your life. In my personal experience and life mentoring, this has been the way people are seeing positive and life changing results. All previous paths taken have not and will not satisfy or work out your situations nor solve your problems.

APRIL 15

Love never fails. You don't have to be afraid of failure anymore or anything. When you walk in the love of God, you are living the most powerful kind of life there is.

APRIL 16

OVER THE PAST YEAR my greatest desire is to do God's will and align myself with His heart's desire, paying close attention to the things that He is most concerned about. We all have our assignments from God, and it's crucial that each of us find our specific assignment whatever that might be. It's key that you persist in asking Him what your assignment is, staying wide open to what He says in reply. Personally I'm willing to go where He tells me to go and pay any price that it will cost. It will take spiritual maturity to hear, accept, and act on what God is saying beyond our immediate needs. If you are unable or unwilling, ask the Holy Spirit to help you align with the heart of God, regardless of the cost, until He becomes the most important thing in your life. Stepping up to such boldness will only yield blessings in your life and the lives of others you will affect because of your obedience to Him.

APRIL 17

I want to invite you to consider investing in others for your own future. If you want genuine and bona fide friends, for example, be a friend to someone who is lonely. Invest in the areas where you want to see a harvest in your life and start expecting blessings to overflow in your life in those areas.

APRIL 18

My prayer for you tonight as you sleep is that "God will tell you the words you need to hear."

APRIL 19

MEDITATE ON THIS TODAY...let go of your self-efforts and rest in the truth that whatever the blessing or success you need, you already have. Believe it, rest in it and see God's blessings manifest in your life.

APRIL 20

Take time to have some fun this coming weekend! Take time to dance, go to a yard sale, go on a hike, get a haircut, color your hair, get a manicure, walk a scenic trail, go see a movie, go to a ballgame, take a yoga class, work out at the gym, work out outside, even do some baking. And, the list can go on and on. Do things that will be fun and that will bring joy and happiness to your life. The great part about this list is some of the suggestions don't even require money.

APRIL 21

Tonight, count your blessings instead of your problems. As you do this, you will begin to experience happiness and joy.

APRIL 22

IF YOU WOULD TRUST ME and do this next exercise, things will start to move in your favor. Repeat out loud as many times as you can "SOMETHING GOOD IS HAPPENING TO ME NOW!"

APRIL 23

Today, expect God to counsel and instruct you about the things in your life, both big and small.

APRIL 24

JOY is what darkness wants to take from you. Joy is positive energy that flows from one person to the other. If darkness can take away your joy, then it has won. You don't have to give into darkness. ON PURPOSE, chose to be happy, have joy, a good and positive attitude, and walk in divine love. Your affirmation and confession is: "All is well in your life and your soul!"

APRIL 25

You will find God's whispers are admonishing, some are correcting, some are filled with delight and some bring challenges our way. Yet, the net results remain the same. We are to move ourselves toward God in all things. God is our Source, our Protection, our Provider.

APRIL 26

Your tongue is only an instrument. Your heart is where the key lies. Whatever is in your heart in abundance is what will come out your mouth. If you fill your heart with LOVE, then words of LOVE will come out of your mouth.

APRIL 27

When we come to God with all of our imperfections, we will never hear Him say "You are not deserving of spending time with Me!" No, He will call us by name and say, "Let's go to your place. I want to chill and hang out with you."

APRIL 28

Just one word of God's wisdom can change your entire situation. Just one word from His mouth can break that lifelong destructive dependency, restore that broken relationship or give you an extraordinary business idea. You don't have to understand God completely for your life to be successful each day. However, you must spend personal, quality, and one-on-one time with Him every day. Include your children in this practice, too!

APRIL 29

If we will put the Word Of God into our hearts and minds on a continual basis, then it will become a habit, making it easy to trust

God and effortless to receive His Son Jesus. His is risen and He is alive.

APRIL 30

LET THIS REVELATION sink into your heart. God is your source, your protection, your provision. He is with you to the very end.

May 1

God knows about all your challenges, including your weaknesses. If an error you've made keeps coming back to haunt you, or if you have a weakness that keeps showing up, don't focus on it and get frustrated. Look through God's eyes and see as He sees you—by His grace. God's grace will get you through it all.

May 2

God seeks us out so that He can encourage and motivate us to keep moving forward, to our next stage, in the life He has planned for us, and it's marvelous!

May 3

We cannot hurry the move of God in our lives. We stay, we soak in His presence. We wait patiently. The answers will come.

May 4

My personal experience with meeting, talking, and visiting with individuals from all walks of life, I have come to the following conclusion: the most important thing I see that people need more than anything is the LOVE OF GOD. God's love lives in my soul. As I move about and around people, praying as I move, that all will receive, that their souls will become open, wanting this precious love that lives on my inside. Yes, I give it to them. It is the LOVE OF GOD!

MAY 5
When we let go of our self-efforts and totally depend on God's grace, He will take over and do in us and through us what we cannot do for ourselves!

MAY 6
Prayer for today: "That God will cause your paths to cross with that of the right people who will be a blessing to you and to whom you can be a blessing!"

MAY 7
Get up tomorrow, go to work or do whatever you do, putting one foot in front of the other and remembering that God is with you. The next day, do the same thing again. God and you are going to get through this together. But it will only happen one day at a time.

MAY 8
This is a very simple post...I'm alive TODAY! I'm able to move about and around with my body. I have a good, strong mind. I have shelter and food to eat. I have clothes and shoes to wear. I am so grateful and thankful for this day. A day that I have never seen before nor will ever see again. I believe we all can share these words together.

May 9

Today is a good day to meditate on the following words: "I am loved by God." Every day you should personalize, practice, and rest in God's love for you. Expect great things to happen when you believe that God loves you in an intimate and personal way.

May 10

TODAY...reward yourself with something fun, something exciting, something that will make your heart sing and your spirit smile. It's time to be nice to YOU!

May 11

Has fear attacked you about during what God has put in your heart to do or become? Let me encourage you. Fear may be saying to you "You can't" or "You don't have the ability." Change your mindset and thoughts by saying "I can, I have the ability, and I'm going to do what God has called me to do!"

May 12

THERE IS A SECRET TO...getting ahead. If you would make a decision to spend twenty minutes, three times a day, for the next thirty days, meditating on being grateful for the things that are well in your life, you will experience such an impact on your life that you could never imagine.

MAY 13

THIS ONE THING I'M POSITIVE ABOUT...is this: whatever door God opens next, I will run through it in faith!

MAY 14

DECIDE TODAY...that what God has called you to be is what you are, and that is what you are supposed to be doing! And, you are supposed to be good at it and successful at it.

MAY 15

There is just one thing you utterly can't afford to do without and that is your time spent in meditation, prayer, and being in the presence of God. It is your very life. It is where your victory comes from. Don't fall for the time-stealers that come your way. Stay alert, and don't get side tracked by them. Make the time you spend with God your first priority every day.

MAY 16

Today, make a choice to stop stressing about your health, finances, family, career or whatever is troubling you. Do your part by what needs to be done and pass the matter to God, trusting Him to guide you. God cares for you and loves you deeply. Make a DECISION TODAY.

May 17

There will be days that are more challenging than others. Days that give you a feeling of being overwhelmed. Don't try to feel your way through the challenges, but use your faith purposefully and wait patiently for the answer. Remind yourself you have been down this road before. And God brought you through without fail. His promises are yet true!

May 18

Allow your actions to have a measurable impact on the world. Be willing to stand up for what you believe in instead of looking the other way. You have the ability to provide a positive perspective to the world that can provide and promote values and maybe even foster lasting change in their lives.

May 19

If this present generation ever succeeds in doing that BIG thing, that GREAT thing, that UNSPEAKABLE thing that GOD purposes that we should do, it will only be when we enter into that DIVINE compassion of God.

May 20

When the storms of life are upon and around us, if we will just stop right in the middle of it all and GIVE THANKS, it will keep us standing strong. Thanksgiving keeps us connected to God and receiving from Him even when circumstances are dark.

May 21

TODAY...expect doors to start opening and your dreams to start becoming reality.

May 22

God's plan for you is BIG and it is absolutely perfect. Find out what it is. Take time to become still, listen to Him every day. Then, whatever He says to you, do it!

May 23

Most of our challenges are ones we anticipate or fear are coming tomorrow. How many people are so concerned about the things of today? Our world is in a state of dismay concerning tomorrow, or the next day, or the next day. Don't be concerned about tomorrow. Rest in God. HIs mighty arms will carry you tomorrow, just as they did today.

May 24

In the mist of all the pain, with an act of obedience, let us express gratitude to God...BY FAITH!

May 25

When you don't know what else to do but turn to God, that's generally when God's miracle-working power can begin to operate in you in the greatest way. With God, there's no such thing as a hopeless situation. That corner you are backed into right now can become a place of new beginnings! People all around you are struggling right now. They are hearing voices, telling them that they won't make it, but they will if they focus their attention on God, and you will, too! Your victory probably will not come as you thought, but believe this: God is with you, and He will get you through whatever it is you're facing if you'll surrender and seek Him.

May 26

When you do the one thing that is required, you will end up doing the right thing at the right time, and God will cause all that you touch to be amazingly blessed!

My 27

There will be a time you feel that your faith has run its course. When that time comes, take notice of how God has been faithful in your past and believe He will be faithful NOW in your present. Trust the fact that God remains faithful even when we are wavering in FAITH.

May 28

In the eyes of God, it doesn't matter what has happened in your past. He doesn't scrutinize it, and neither should you. Make a choice NOW that you will look forward to better days and better things. Believe and trust that God has a better and brighter future in store for you.

May 29

It's time for our society as a whole to learn how to be calm, take a slower pace in life, relax and step back and away from the stress-induced "fight or flight" reaction so many are used to.

May 30

REMEMBER...God's plan for our FUTURE far exceeds anything we could ever come up with on our own.

May 31

We not only cheat ourselves, we cheat everyone we come in contact with when we don't live and walk in the love of God. When His love is manifested, people change, and their lives are forever altered. People are ready and waiting for you to show up in their lives with unconditional love: the love of God. You can start NOW!

JUNE 1

Expressing gratitude will change everything around you. It will change the whole complexion of your life. Today, we are thankful.

JUNE 2

I am determined to be a light to the world. I am determined to live such a life, showing others the light of God, so that they will want this same light in their lives! Who wants to join me?

JUNE 3

Your next weekend, I encourage you to play, have fun, spend time with family and friends, seek to help others experience happiness. Showing gratitude, compassion, and love to others will not only bring happenings to others but will help the world become a better place, with you being part of that change. Yes, you can make a difference.

JUNE 4

Remind yourself that no matter what your situations are, it could be worse. You are still alive!

JUNE 5

Whatever challenges you have today, remember God's love for you. Make a conscious, personal decision to meditate on His love for you instead of the negative forces against you. That's how you CONQUER THE GIANTS in your life!

JUNE 6

IF YOU FIND YOURSELF FEELING...stress today. The good news is you don't have to fly to a remote island or find a meditation center to find release.

1. Find a comfortable chair, sit down as you normally would.
2. Leave your feet flat on the floor.
3. Sit up straight.
4. Relax your shoulders.
5. Allow your arms to rest on your legs.
6. Palms facing up or down, close your eyes.
7. INHALE, pause, EXHALE, pause.
8. Repeat four times.

JUNE 7

Don't try to figure it all out. If you do, you will just mess it up. All you need to do is trust God in every situation. Each day wake up expecting God's favor in and upon your life. Then you see God show up and make up any difference in every area of your life!

JUNE 8

Here is how to have a great day, every day! The moment you wake up on a daily basis is a gift from God. It should be started with thanksgiving before you get out of the bed. Make the decision to start this day and every day afterward spending time with God when you get out of bed: do it before you start with Twitter, Facebook, Instagram, and any other social media.

JUNE 9

If you have a challenging situation in your life today, know that God is interested in getting you out of them. Even if it was a result of something you did without wisdom, God doesn't hold it against you. God will not ask whose fault it was or why you did what you did. He is only interested in solving your problem. Today, bring your situation before Him, seek His provision and He will give you the wisdom and the means to clear everything!

JUNE 10

BEFORE BED TONIGHT...count your blessings!

JUNE 11

Today, make a decision not to allow strife to enter your spirit. Ask God to help you to notice it immediately and to overcome it. Determine to resist it. Say the affirmation "I will walk in the peace of God." As you move into this direction, you will discover how wonderful life can be.

JUNE 11

Breakthroughs come and amazing things begin to happen to you when you truly believe how much God loves YOU!

JUNE 12

Only what we do for God will last throughout eternity. It is vital that we all be about the business of what He called us to do.

Everything and anything outside of His plan for our lives is inconsequential, both in the spiritual and physical realm.

June 13

YOU MAY FEEL AT TIMES THAT DIFFICULTIES HAVE BEEN CREATED...in your endeavor to fulfill your calling in life, but don't be discouraged. Those obstacles are only temporary. The only way something can steal your dream, vision, or calling is if you surrender to it first! If you hold on and refuse to give up, your faith will overcome every hindrance that is in your path!

June 14

God is more concerned with what's in your heart than in your natural abilities, skills, education, "know-how," or looks. Your heart is the first priority to God. Make it a point to keep your heart soft and flexible to the callings of God in your life.

June 15

Meditation for today: "God's love never fails. It never gives up. It never runs out."

June 16

Choose wisely the people you call friends and surround yourself with. Trust God to give you faith-filled friends who will lift you up when you are down and give you divine counsel and inspire you to go ahead, follow, and accomplish your God-given dreams. My prayer for you that you will begin to have a grateful and thankful heart toward God for all His blessings in your life, including your divine friends and relationships!

June 17
WHEN YOU COME TO THE END OF YOUR LIFE...your success in life will be determined in one question: did you do what God called you to do?

June 18
MY PRAYER FOR YOU...today is that "you will be the messengers of God's love, telling men, women, children, people everywhere, that God loves them. That you will demonstrate His love, reaching out to them in their time of need, walking with them and sharing the truth of His love with them. That you will be His love in ACTION."

June 19
Be more interested in long-term success. Don't turn to quick fixes for overnight success. This kind of success may come with a terrible price. Seek success that will last a lifetime. Don't be hasty. Take the time to look at every situation through the eyes of LOVE. Spend time in meditation and prayer: this is where your firm foundation will develop with wisdom and success.

June 20
SOMEWHERE IN THE WORLD...someone needs you to pray for them. Spend some time praying for others today.

June 21
I WANT TO CHALLENGE…you starting now. Don't allow one negative word to come out of your mouth throughout the weekend. Place your hand over your mouth if you have to, or even bite your tongue. If you do happen to say negative words, apologize and keep moving forward.

June 22
Meditation for tonight…"Here I am Lord. Here I am. All my hope is in you!"

June 23
Today, take five, ten, or fifteen minutes to be still. Make sure you are alone and in a quiet place. Don't have any expectations. This quiet time will enrich your life. It will enable you to enjoy whatever you do in your life more fully and cheerfully.

June 24
NO MATTER WHAT…your situations might look like, you can experience real, positive change when you look to God.

June 25
MY PRAYER FOR YOU…today is "That you believe God is on your side. That He is for you and not against you. That He will help you make every decision you need to make. That you will trust Him to show you the best possible decision every time."

JUNE 26

Take time today to be still, to meditate and to pray, and watch God direct you to success!

JUNE 27

NEXT WEEKEND...remember, there is no one in the world like YOU. Your genetic makeup is unique to you only. No other fingerprints are like yours in the world. Your eye color, your blood type, your biological makeup: all of these are exclusive and special to you. There is not another human being on the face of the earth just like you. You are truly one of a kind.

JUNE 28

To realize that you can make an impact on someone else's life should be a "WOW" moment for you. Having such opportunities to inspire people is an honor.

JUNE 29

Victory is inevitable for you and for me, if we will stay in FAITH and not quit.

JUNE 30

The relationship that exists between you and God is precious! God is deeply in love with you. Just as someone in love thinks about, dreams of, and cherishes the one they love, God longs for you, thinks about you, desires to be close to you, and wants to reveal Himself to you.

July 1

The times when you are discouraged, it's good to hit the rewind button in your mind and go back to earlier experiences with God when faith was simple and life was uncomplicated. Do you remember how precious those days were? Do you recall how changed you were by the power of God? Do you remember the joy and laughter you experienced? It's good for you to rehearse those experiences because they will stir you up, encourage you, and bring strength for the battle you are facing right now.

July 2

YOU WILL FIND THAT...as you continue to seek the will of God for your life, you will have many types of attacks and challenges that come with being OBEDIENT. And you will have desires and thoughts to "run the other way" and get away from the pressure of obeying God! Your mind and body would enjoy "a getaway" to somewhere else where FAITH is not required. Stand your ground. Your seasons of harvest are about to appear.

July 3

The number one thing about faith: it never gives up.

July 4

Happy July 4th! As we remember and celebrate Independence Day, my prayer is that God will continue to preserve America. We know our forefathers sacrificed so much, had so much patience, and yet knew they needed to rely on God for our independence. Today, we must continue the same. Today, we celebrate July 4th with parades and fireworks, yet, let us also include making time to be grateful and give thanks to God for His continual blessings upon our country!

July 5

YOU'LL FIND THAT...when you surround yourself with like-minded individuals, your faith will erupt and you will see major breakthroughs in your life!

July 6

FAITH IS DESIGNED...by God to change things. Faith will move mountains. Faith will bring God's promises to fruition in your life. Faith will bring you victory! Today, if you need things changed and mountains moved in your life, use your faith purposefully and receive the promises God has for you!

July 7

TODAY...I am praying over you, declaring you will be the overcomer you were born into God's family to be and that your faith in God will manifest in every area of your life and ministry.

July 8

YOUR WORDS...create the spiritual atmosphere in your life, either good or bad.

July 9

Your next weekend is going to be another great weekend! Do at least one FUN thing today for YOURSELF! It could be taking a yoga class, going to the movies, enjoying a great meal with family and/or friends, or just being lazy around your home.

July 10

Don't allow negative thoughts and voices tell you that you are insignificant, unimportant, and that others view you as being small. God sees you as a significant and important part of His master plan. You are BIG in His eyes. God needs you to fulfill your destiny, and other people are depending and waiting on you to show up in their lives.

July 11

Today, allow JOY to stay in the present moment. That's the only moment where God's love can be found. Today make each moment count.

July 12

MY PRAYER FOR YOU TODAY...that "God will instruct, show, and teach you the way you should go. That you will know He Is guiding you and watching over you. You will receive His solution to all your problems."

July 13

At the end of it all, saying affirmations are good, meditation is good, being positive is good. Yet, all these things will not get you to where you need to be spiritually. You need the mighty working power of God living on the inside. This power, this relationship, this coming into fellowship with God is the only solution to your situation and the world. You just don't need to know of Jesus, you need to really know Him.

July 14

When you walk in love of God, you will forget past hurts and mistakes. When someone asks you for forgiveness, you forgive and you let it go!

July 15

You can come to the place in your spiritual walk that you give all your problems, troubles, and situations to God. You come to the place that you quit trying to solve them yourself. Because, realistically, if you could have taken care of them, you would have already. Today, release them all to God. Let Him take care of you. The battle is His, not yours. Take your position, stand firm, and receive His provision and protection.

July 16

You don't have to give in to displeasing emotions in challenging or difficult moments. If you will allow God to work in you, He will release a supernatural joy and a dominating peace from deep down inside of you. This will keep you joyful, calm, stable, and peaceful, even though you are face to face with situations that would normally push you over the edge!

July 17

Know that YOU have a reservoir filled with unbeatable life forces inside you and these forces are ready to come forth. Let them come!

July 18

One of the things I do for individuals when talking to them one on one is give them tools to take back control of their lives. One of the tools involves finding God's Master Plan for their lives. Only then will they experience complete satisfaction in all they do.

July 19

Today, I will keep an attitude of faith and expectancy.

July 20

In order to have complete freedom, you will have to have your mind renewed daily by the Word of God. Renewing your mind with the Word of God replaces the wrong and negative thinking with right believing thinking. This is one of the first major commitments you must do in order to have a freedom which agrees with what the Word of God declares you to be.

July 21

Daily, tell God you need Him to be your partner (senior partner) in all of your personal and business dealings. Doing this, making God your partner, will always keep you employed.

July 22

There will be times in your life that you "miss it" when it comes to making decisions or choices in life. Whatever the decisions or choices were does not mean you didn't hear God's voice, nor took the necessary time to get confirmation. Not to worry, because of God's amazing love for us, there is a way out. Simply ask God for help, then believe He will get you through it all with expectations beyond what you could ever possibly imagine.

July 23

One of your daily meditations and prayers should be praying that God will cause you to ever excel, increase, and overflow in His love.

July 24

If we want to enjoy everything God has for us, we must trust Him in every area of our lives.

July 25

Do you know that what is not love is fear! Every negative emotion you experience derives from fear not love. When you allow yourself to feel fear, your judgment undergoes an extraordinary transformation, which is not good. When this happens, you have no power to service people. You cannot communicate with them in a meaningful way. Fear brings this on and can bring on more harm if you don't release it and step back into love.

July 26

Make a decision to put aside your ideas and seek God's wisdom in all things pertaining to your life! You will find it to be the only thing that can permanently solve the problems before you. This is one of the most precious gift God has to give.

July 27

Today, lets make a commitment to encourage and love others where they are right now in their lives.

July 28

First thing each morning when you wake up and before your feet touch the floor...acknowledge God. Thank Him for allowing you to see a day you have never seen before, nor will ever see again. Then, take a few minutes to pray for three individuals that come to mind. Afterward, say this affirmation *"Something great is happening to me right now!"* Not only will this ground you for the new day, but it also gives you an opportunity to clear away whatever happened the day or night before and start fresh. I know this sounds pretty simple, but it is true.

July 29

Do what you have to do regarding your life and situations, but refuse to worry and live each day like a child.

July 30

Forgiveness requires an act of faith on your part. You cannot do it on your own natural ability. It is a supernatural ability where you must use your faith on purpose for the love of God to come in and totally erase the incident from your consciousness. Today make the quality decision to forgive by an act of your will. Forgive, get free and free others, too.

JULY 31
Love, as a matter of fact, goes out of the way to make sure people are not hurt. In other words, love not does not cause hurt.

August 1

Being neutral about things will eventually cause great challenges in your life. You will begin to lose ground with your faith, not being able to hold on to and accomplish your God-given dreams and goals. That inner spiritual drive and momentum will soon leave. Instead of being strong in the Lord, you become weak in your faith, ultimately losing any hold you had in God helping you accomplish your goals.

August 2

Slow it down, take some time today, CONSIDER and MEDITATE on this..."When you become connected to God, you won't see yourself in failure any longer."

August 3

If you will hold on to what you know spiritually (God's knowledge and revelations), fight and stand your ground right where you are, you will not be destroyed! The victory will be yours!

August 4

God is not moved by need. He is only moved by our faith in Him and our ability to receive.

August 5

By Jesus's own acts, He gave the world the map for individual and world peace along with salvation. If you accept His teaching, way of life and instructions, it will change your life forever. The main focus then becomes "loving one another as He loved us."

August 6

There is no substitute for the love of God (Christ living in us). We do have the capacity to love. When we step back from walking in our natural abilities and let the Spirit of God come forth, we will see complete healing in all areas of people we come in contact with. I so desire to be in the group of individuals who will manifest the real love of God all the time to all the people.

August 7

Your weekend is here! I want to suggest you do at least three fun things this weekend.

Just a few ideas:

Paint your nails	Take a walk	See a movie
Give someone a hug	Watch the sun set	Take a bubble bath
Eat cotton candy	Ride your bike	Go to the zoo
Write a book	Play mini golf	Visit a museum
Have breakfast in bed	Dance like no one is looking	

August 8

Slow it down, take some time today, CONSIDER and MEDITATE on this…"When you become connected to God, you won't see yourself in failure any longer."

August 9

You might have lived much of your life facing failure after failure, however, my prayer for you this Sunday evening is that "God will meet you right where you are in life, quickly turn it around, and usher you into His abundant favor."

August 10

Out of our mouths we have the ability to either bless or curse. We can bless the name and work of God, and in our next sentence, we can speak evil of others. This should not be. Today, speak words of faith, having kind words toward people, thereby blessing them.

August 11

Whatever situation or problem you are faced with, I want to encourage you to have faith in God to stay the course, pray until God works it out. Let your affirmation and confession be: "Something great is happening to me RIGHT NOW!"

August 12

Today, make yourself a list of just five things that excite you. Don't get into the details. After you create the list, immediately find ways to integrate each one into your daily or weekly routine. In doing this you will find yourself going through life in a wave of total excitement that will lift you up along with others. They will then see, as you will see, that life is worth living!

AUGUST 13

If you are feeling run down, bored, with no energy to do what you are currently doing with your life, you are probably not doing what you are called to do. Take time to be quiet, see what is in your spirit, your heart. It may take a prayer, meditation time, reading the Word, to gain the clarity you need. It will be worth the effort, time, and wait! When clear direction comes, don't ask for others' opinions on what God revealed to you. When you truly know what you are supposed to do, just do it.

AUGUST 14

You can become addicted to loving people unconditionally. All you have to do is make a decision to do it. Let God do the rest. Once you do, you will never be willing to live without doing it.

AUGUST 15

There will be times where you will want to ask others to give you answers to your problem. That would be the easy way out. If others give you answers to your problems, you might enjoy success for a while, but another situation will come along and what will you do? Buckle down, do your own praying, ask God for direction. Become disciplined to start searching out the things of God: this is where your permanent answers are.

AUGUST 16

Today, take just a moment and stop looking at your situation. You look in the mirror, and you see an unqualified and inexperienced individual who can't do anything right. But let me remind you your disqualifications only exist in your mind. You are loved, are special, are extraordinary in the eyes of God. You live, move, and have your very being in the power of God! You have Him with you 100 percent of the time. You are a success, prosperous, and well able to do all the things God has called you to do and has said what you are. You depend on Him. God is your source, your provision, and your protection. As you confess and begin to believe these words and statements, before long people will begin to take notice that you are indeed blessed by God.

AUGUST 17
God loves it when you draw from His endless supply of favor, grace, mercy, peace, strength, and wisdom.

AUGUST 18
Because we are spiritual beings, living in this physical body, everything is spiritual and manifests in the natural or physical world. All answers to our circumstances, problems, and situations can be found in the spiritual realm. God is waiting for you and I to consult Him regarding them all. His Holy Spirit will direct, lead, and guide you to all truth and to victory in every area in your life, spiritually and physically. Make the time to communicate daily or as often as you need with God, following the advise of the Holy Spirit. You can never go wrong doing this.

AUGUST 19
That there will never be a need in your life that cannot be met 100 percent, in abundance, and overflowing by the grace of God!

AUGUST 20

There will be times in your life that you will feel and believe that God is a million miles away. These will be the dark times in our lives, where we feel alone. Let me encourage you that there is nowhere in the world, the universe, etc. that we cannot be covered by God's favor, mercy, grace, and wisdom. He is God when we are on the mountaintops, as well when we are in the valley—know that! Don't give up nor give in to defeat. God has and will not leave us alone...He is our strength, especially in the valley.

AUGUST 21

Rejoice! Knowing that whatever our circumstances are today, we can find peace in God's Word and His Son Jesus. He is called the Prince of Peace, even through the most serious and chaotic times of our lives. How do you find this peace? See Him morning, noon, and night without fail, believing and trusting He will bring you out of all your troubles, making you whole, with nothing missing and nothing broken.

AUGUST 22

The Bible is full of true stories of how God's presence was with individuals during the stormy and trying times of their lives, even almost unto death. These individuals didn't look at their situations. If they did...they would have been discouraged. They looked to God. Because they did, God delivered them with His mighty hand. We serve the same God who is still in the deliverance and saving business. Look to Him. Expect to see and experience more than you could ever imagine beyond your current situations today!

AUGUST 23

Nothing is more important this very minute than developing your faith in God to supply your every need! Also, know that faith will only work when you are walking in total forgiveness toward others and unconditional love.

AUGUST 24

The Bible states that we are seated RIGHT NOW in heavenly places with Christ Jesus, which means we have direct access to the Father. You can RIGHT NOW ask your Father for what you need and state your desires according to His Master Plan for your life.

AUGUST 25

A lot of the supernatural blessings that God bestows upon us go many times without us recognizing them. Why? Because they were not done in a way that brought about excitement. They were done under the radar. God is ALWAYS doing more for you than darkness will ever do to you!

AUGUST 26

The best person in the world could be certified to teach yoga, elected to a political office, or be ruler of the world, and it wouldn't do one bit of good if the people did not awaken to God.

AUGUST 27

God has chosen us to go through certain experiences so we can help others. Those experiences come for us to be a witness, teacher, and leader for others, moving us all to the point where we will be in position to meet the need of "souls" who would otherwise stay defeated and discouraged. Today, August 27, the year of our Lord, be encouraged and strengthened, and you will comfort others.

August 28

Daily, we should seek God about where to go and who to talk to... giving those individuals hope, faith, and the realization that God loves them so much! The words you will bring to them will give them the rest in their soul that is so needed.

August 29

The more we study God's Word, the more we seek His will; there will always be opportunities to follow Him closer, to know Him deeper. We can become like a child, soaking and absorbing, grasping the mind of God. As we continue to move into this place, there will come a time that darkness will not be able to tell the difference between us and God Himself.

August 30

If you, for the next twenty-one days, would repeat, "Something great is happening to me right now!" several times a day...your life will be more prosperous, spiritually, mentally, and physically after the twenty-one days.

AUGUST 31

Today, you are facing a situation where you see no solutions, none at all. All options seem impossible. However, God can change your situation in the blink of any eye. Give Him a way into your life. Go to Him, start a conversation, a relationship, a fellowship with Him. He will give you a way out (you only need one) of ALL your impossible circumstances, along with solutions to ALL your situations. In the end, you will be able to say not in faith, but as a reality, "All is well in my life and my soul!"

SEPTEMBER 1

In all situations, problems, and circumstances, we should always "rest in God." We are to spiritually rest in God regarding all things, not taking the burdens of them nor fretting and worrying about them. We keep doing what we know to do, moving forward with our lives, resting in Him, knowing He (God) is our Source, Provision, and Protection. This is what freedom is all about.

SEPTEMBER 2

Your trials may be fiery, intense, severe, and overpowering...know that our God whom we serve is able to deliver you and He will deliver you...because there is no other God who can deliver like Him!

SEPTEMBER 3

When you come to the point that you want to leave the vicious loop of defeat and failures in your life...the answer is going to be seeing yourself as God sees you because of the work of Christ on the cross. Through this process there is no condemnation, guilt, or shame. There are only the blessings of God and unconditional love throughout eternity.

SEPTEMBER 4

Come to the place in your life, your soul...one in which you will hear, listen, and act according to the whispers of God. Those whispers will prompt you to be at certain places, at appointed times, with words to speak that will minister to, bring healing, and even save a person's physical and spiritual life. Let God use you!

SEPTEMBER 5

As a child of God, one of the most devastating things you can do is to get comfortable and satisfied, believing you have made it, becoming lazy in the matters of the spirit such as studying the Word, praying, saying affirmations, and meditation of scriptures.

SEPTEMBER 6

Today...God is looking for individuals whose hearts are perfect toward Him. God has been doing this since the beginning of time and has not stopped. He looks at our hearts, not at our outward appearance. Today, let God find your heart perfect toward Him!

SEPTEMBER 7

Don't attach your mind to the things everyone else is doing; stay focused on the things God has called you to do. Finish those things with joy because they are pleasing to our God, our Father. As you set and keep your eyes on the prize, nothing will be able to keep you from finishing your course.

SEPTEMBER 8

It's so precious to God when we don't worry about things and just trust Him.

SEPTEMBER 9

A simple prayer that you can pray daily is to ask God to give you opportunities to minister into the lives of kids, for them to meet God in a very real way, wanting to impact them in a way that not only celebrates their eternity but also equips them with spiritual tools they need to battle with darkness they face daily...AND WIN!

September 10
Every day, we can go into our quiet time, our meditation time, or our prayer time and pray for the many (some by name) whose children need a personal encounter with God. There should never be a price too big and no effort too great to make sure the next generation will grow up with the knowledge and strength of God.

September 11
Our trials, tribulations, challenges, hardships, setbacks, etc. do not define who we are. We are the righteous (in right standing with God) of God because of what Jesus did on the cross. Believe that God is with you. Believe that you are on the right path. Believe that God is your Source, your Provision, and your Protection.

September 12
Tomorrow, September 13th, I want you to get up, have the love of God in your heart, serve Him with everything you've got, be the best person you can possibly be, love people, help people, do what you know to be a representative for God. Think about the many ways you can be a blessing.

September 13
Even though God's love for us is eternal and unconstitutionally, a life of not walking in His love toward others brings about a cost.

It will rob us of faith and cause us to be filled with doubts, fear, unbelief, and keep our prayers from being answered. Don't allow this to happen. Make the commitment that you are going to do the things that are pleasing to God.

SEPTEMBER 14
Each day you wake up, what if you asked God to allow you to fall in love with people all over again? Oh, what a different world this would be.

SEPTEMBER 15
My prayer for you today is "that you are blessed in all things pertaining to your life, including spirit, soul, and body. And that no bodily harm or danger will come near you. I pray everything you do will be successful."

SEPTEMBER 16
No matter what the circumstances, pray and speak God's blessing over those who you consider to be negative toward you, have an evil intent toward you, or that you consider to be your enemy. As you pray and speak God's blessings over them, you are asking God to open their heart to them to receive His unconditional love, His plan, and His will for their lives.

SEPTEMBER 17
Whatever you believe, speak and agree with will be established or come to pass. The circumstances will follow your actions and

affirmations. Today, make the decision and let your affirmations be that you are financially secure, healed, healthy, well, and will live a long and satisfying life, just to name a few.

September 18

As you approach the weekend, schedule some time to just "soak" in the presence of God, with this affirmation: "God I trust You."

September 19

Never lose sight of the fact that you are a part of the solution to the problems we face as human beings. God has not given you, me, or anyone else a revelation or truth so special that it is only for a handful to believe they are above helping and loving people unconditional. As you prepare for your upcoming week tell your mind and body: the reality is this…get busy loving and serving others!

September 20

Take time this week to make space for God to come into your home, life, family, circumstances, job, business, and other areas of your life. When you do, there will be a miracle waiting.

September 21

Don't give up on your dreams. Choose to believe they will become a reality. Don't become lazy in your prayer time, your meditation, and your affirmations. Hold on and don't let go. You will be glad you did!

SEPTEMBER 22

You have to believe when God has called you beyond the POINT OF NO RETURN, He has a plan waiting for you that will exceed your wildest dreams and imagination.

SEPTEMBER 23

Many of you have found "the path" that now brings success to everything you do. I want to encourage you to consider making time for anyone that wants to know how you got there. Let this be just one of the ways you give back to society.

SEPTEMBER 24

Today, I encourage you begin the practice of giving and showing grace to others, allowing words of exhortation to come out of your mouth, and using your words to encourage others, along with keeping a mindset of forgiveness, one for another. These are things that will help increase your love in the ways of God.

SEPTEMBER 25

Don't allow the physical world to have the final word regarding your life. Don't just believe what you can feel and see in the physical. Come into agreement with what God says. Look to the Spirit for your need and desires. When you do, you will begin to have victories in all areas of your life.

September 26

Every situation will be different. I want to encourage you to ask God for grace and mercy and to forgive and love the people who have done you wrong or said unkind things to you. Do you know for certain if they really meant to do or to say those things, or what was going on in their lives when it happened?

September 27

There will be times in your life that circumstances and situations will compel you to react or respond to them. These are times you should especially listen to the Spirit as what to do. If you react or respond without the prompting of the Spirit, you could cause more problems, troubles, with no solution available.

September 28

There will be times in your life that in order for the wisdom of God to appear...you will have to get quiet and be still. Only after you have done this will the answers and wisdom come forth.

September 29

Irritations and aggravations are two of the worst enemies you will face in this life. Though you have the power to overcome the works of darkness, if you are not consistent in things of the spirit and body, you will eventually fall prey to these works. You do have the ability and power within you to move from the valley of doubt and defeat to the mountaintop with right believing, living in total prosperity (spirit, soul, body).

SEPTEMBER 30

If God is leading you to do something, you can know without a doubt He has a good reason for it. He sees and knows what you cannot see. If you will follow God's direction, He will take you exactly where you need to go and help you reach your maximum potential in life.

October 1

When you are led by God to take a step of faith, to do something new, you might just get a little shaken up. Don't give it a second thought, these are only temporary feelings. God has your back.

October 2

No matter what your circumstances, you are not alone, God is with you. Find individuals full of faith that will encourage you and tell you that you can and will overcome all obstacles. In the midst of all things, find space to be grateful and thankful for the present moment.

October 3

Building relationships with the right people allows you to work together, whether physically or spiritually, to increase each other's capacity to accomplish greater things than either of you could do alone. Move forward with your passion, never looking back and knowing all is well.

October 4

Try this: every day of the week, a minimum of three times a day until you go to bed, set your alarm. When the alarm goes off, stop what you are doing and say the following twenty-two times: "Bless Your Name God." Something this simple will keep negative thoughts at bay.

October 5

Take time each day to thank God for the small things in your life He did for you that no one else knows about.

OCTOBER 6

Today, this week, this year, the rest of your life…look for opportunities to become involved with the poor. Becoming involved with "the poor" will include any person under any kind of oppression who needs the freedom of God shown to them. Examples can be individuals who are lonely, hurting from emotional abuse, grief from the loss of a loved one, financially stressed and depressed, or simply needing someone to pray for them. It's time for us to show people we care.

OCTOBER 7

There have been many times I have been faced with situations that looked impossible, and I was tempted to give up. But I didn't quit. If I had let go of my faith, I would have missed God. In all those times, there was no source for me to depend on but God. And no matter how bad things looked, God has never failed me.

OCTOBER 8

You have to forgive others when they miss it, and you have to forgive yourself when you miss it in some area of your life. If you don't do both, you will be crippled and deprived for the rest of your life.

OCTOBER 9

I encourage you to never let go of the fact that God is your source. Stop looking at your paycheck, your bank account, or what you think people can do for you. These are not your source. Do what I do every day. Make it a habit to say the following prayer: "God, You are my source and I expect miracles today." Live your life in this manner. Expect God's blessings and miracles, and you will not feel like giving up.

OCTOBER 10

Do you want everything to be well in your life? Do you want to be empowered by God? Do you want to be a mighty force of God? Then take an hour or two out of the twenty-four hours in a day and spend that time with God. If you do, your entire life will change as a result. One year from the moment you start, God's presence will be so powerful in your life that you will no longer have to say by faith, "All is well in my life." You will say it because it's now a reality. Something to think about STARTING TOMORROW MORNING.

OCTOBER 11

Today, know that God loves you and is here for you.

OCTOBER 12

If you have not been there yet...somewhere down the road, you will come to a point of no return in your life. This is the time you go to God and let Him be your Source, Protection, and Provision. In God, nothing is impossible, and we can move forward with confidence, past the point of no return.

OCTOBER 13

Do you have morning quiet time? What do you say to people you meet today? It might come to you right away or it might come as you are preparing to get ready for the day. But the word they need will come for you to share and change their lives from the inside out.

October 14

As you allow God's love to grow in you, you will find that people want to be near you because you create such an enjoyable experience for them. Once they absorb this love that is evident in your life, they will want to come back over and over again to experience more of this yummy love in you!

October 15

I want to encourage you to not think nor talk about your problems. This weekend, take one day, or even just one hour, to enjoy your life. Talking and thinking about your financial problems, your relationship problems, or your health problems will not solve them. Give them to God. Let Him do what He does best: taking care of you.

October 16

God desires to bless you, to surround you with goodwill, to always protect you. I encourage you today, October 16, to receive the blessing, receive the goodwill, and receive the protection.

October 17

There is only ONE you can trust 100 percent all of the time. He has never failed me and will never fail you: and that is our GOD! Rest and trust Him.

October 18

Today, make it a goal to "love on purpose" people you come in contact with. Before you leave home, ask God to open your spiritual eyes for individuals who need this the most. Then, ask God to open their eyes and ears to the unconditional love of God, giving them a way of escape from whatever is holding their lives back.

October 19

Let your meditation and prayer today be: "God, allow me to have an overflow of Your love, that everyone I meet will experience healing for their wounded hearts. Let me be a living example of love."

October 20

When the storms of life approach you…remain strong in what you believe. The storms will eventually move on.

October 21

As you move about your day God sees your compassion for others and your unconditional and labor of love toward them. It's not going unnoticed. Don't stop. Our world needs more individuals JUST LIKE YOU!

October 22

Stay open to receive answers to your prayers and questions at various places and various times of the day that you least expect. Your answers may come while you take a walk in the neighborhood, or while driving in traffic or shopping at the grocery store; they may even come while you are taking a shower. Leave your mind open to receive answers to all your questions at any place and any time. This is God's sense of humor working. I see you smiling!

OCTOBER 23

Be confident in who you are! You are perfect right now in the eyes of God. Take time this weekend to assure others they have what it takes to succeed in life. As you do this, you are planting seeds of stability in their hearts, giving them the confidence to grow and thrive.

OCTOBER 24

I was once asked about how I start my day. Here is a sample: I wake up each morning between 3:30 and 4am. I do one or two yoga stretches before leaving the bed. Before my feet touch the floor, I say a short prayer (thirty to sixty seconds) about my day and individuals that come to mind. I then go to my special place in my home, taking fourteen to twenty-one minutes to read a devotional, meditate, or just be still, listening to the whispers of God. I leave home knowing I will have numerous opportunities to encourage and serve others that day. I hope this is an inspiration for you.

OCTOBER 25

Today, remember you are on the winning side! No matter how long it takes, keep believing until your healing is complete, your money comes in, and your situation changes.

OCTOBER 26

There will always be individuals who will not give in to external pressures. With the overbearing adversities and influences that we now see in our world, we don't have to succumb to them. I encourage you to steadfastly resist the pressure to conform. Whatever it takes, hold fast to your faith in God, His faithfulness, and stay connected to people of STRONG FAITH. Please share with individuals you know that will be inspired and their souls renewed from you sharing this reading for October 26th.

OCTOBER 27

We should say at the beginning of every challenge, in the mist of the challenge, and when the challenge is over…"We trust God, we know God loves us, we know God has a Master Plan for our lives, and we know God is going to take care of our situation." When we purposely repeat these statements, we win.

OCTOBER 28

You will never be satisfied until you are completely doing what you were born to do on this earth. When you accept and move into your calling, only then will complete prosperity manifest itself in your life and the lives of others you are called to, throughout the earth. Today, October 27, I pray and speak God's blessings over you for stepping out and receiving God's provision so you can walk in full manifestation of your mission in life.

OCTOBER 29

Asking God for vengeance and a lightning bolt to strike down someone who has done us wrong is not acting like God. This is not

His nature nor should it be ours. God has great grace and great mercy. This grace and mercy is not just for you only.

OCTOBER 30

When we become stagnant concerning our dreams, our visions, and have stopped pursuing our purpose in life, we move at break-neck speed toward destruction.

OCTOBER 31

Over the years I have learned there is no situation that disqualifies me from praying. Prayer is available for me and for you. You can overcome difficulties and have your prayers answered. There is only one situation where you will not receive help: your refusal to pray.

NOVEMBER 1

I see light in our world, even in the mist of the chaos, the conflicts, the darkness, and the negativity. The light that I see is the light of God living inside each of you. My prayer is for you to receive this revelation: that God lives in you. Anything not connected with His light has no effect on you!

NOVEMBER 2

We have all made some choices in the past that were not good choices. And, that's where they must be left: in the past! Today, live in the present, live in the moment, because God loves and adores you. His plans for you are marvelous and wonderful. Believe this!

NOVEMBER 4

This coming weekend, take the same attitude as small children have. Become creative (again) in having fun. You still have it in you.

NOVEMBER 5

Do you really want to live? Although your answer may be yes, it comes with "buts" and exceptions: but not in this house, but not alone, but not stressed out. You can begin to remove the negative thoughts, and that change starts in your mind. No matter what your situation is, you can find positive reasons to live each day and expect better days to come. A great daily affirmation I use throughout my day is, "Something great is happening to me right now!"

NOVEMBER 6

Tonight, when you go to bed...grab hold to the vision of your dream being accomplished. Sweet dreams!

NOVEMBER 7

Many are sick physically because their souls are contaminated with a lack of forgiveness toward others and situations that have occurred in their lives. Some even show hatred toward others. If this is you, my prayer is that you will make a conscious decision to forgive, allowing the spirit of compassion and the love of God to come into your heart and consume your entire being. Make this decision on purpose. Start experiencing healing in your soul, your body, your relationships, your home, even your finances.

NOVEMBER 8

People are looking for a way out of want and not having enough, a way out of sickness and disease, a way out of living a life full of oppressive traditions. My desire and goal is to destroy those traditions and bring help and hope to a hurting world from what is destroying their lives. Many of you reading this entry for November 7th, have the same desires and goals. Now, is the time to starting doing something about it!

NOVEMBER 9

As you settle down for the night, know that God is a great friend to you and will always be there for you. Tonight, let God be your peace in all things!

November 10

There is no doubt that we are in a season of spiritual revelation. There is a spiritual contest among us that will bring about radical changes in our lives. The company you keep will have an influence on your spiritual walk. Choose your friends wisely. Become close to them who have a pure heart, those who will encourage, inspire, motivate, and keep you accountable in your love walk with God. Expose yourself to their love, their peace, their faith. Let this become you.

November 11

Now is the time to become tuned to the things of the spirit more than ever before. Our future will be different than what we are used to, in so many ways. We should not continue to take things for granted: many things that were there in the past may not be there in our future. Let us depend on God as our source, our provision, and our protection, becoming more independent of the world system. Let us start now to come together and to encourage and love each other like never before.

November 12

As you move from one season of life to the next, your divine circle of God-given friends will always be there to encourage you in your faith and do whatever they can to help push you to the next chapter of your life. They will pray for you and stick by your side, and they will love you unconditionally through your successes and especially through the times you aren't having success. If you don't have this type of divine relationship, consider asking God. I did, and He delivered.

November 13

When we are in conflict with others, believe it or not, this is an opportunity for us to grow in our respect for the other. If you need help with this, ask God how to proceed. The answers are available.

November 14

Don't stop believing. When we stop believing, everything that is not like God will show up in our minds, such as anxiety, doubt, fear, unbelief, and uncertainty just to name a few.

November 15

Many of you hold the keys to unlock victories in individuals' lives. You know how to win. You know how to show individuals the power they already have. You know how to show them where their source and strength lives. You are the ones whose influence can change every person's life in this world. Today, step out and use the power God has given you. You hold the key!

November 16

You can become overwhelmed by things in your life if you try to fix them in the physical world. Stop struggling to overcome those challenges in natural ways. You will only end up in the cycle of being unsuccessful again and again. Go to God for your answers. He knows your challenges, your struggles, and your weakness. God will give you ways to overcome them.

November 17
As you mature more in spiritual things, one of your major goals should be not to complicate things. Answers to your questions should become simpler and clearer for all of your life's situations... they can be easily found in your heart.

November 18
A long time ago, a decision was made for you to live in the physical body you have now. It is no mistake that you are alive and living on this earth, at this present time. It is a great time to be alive, to live and see all that is occurring right before your very eyes. Allow God to use you in areas you were created to thrive in, for the sake of bringing healing to the world.

November 19
THIS MIGHT SOUND EXTREME...but if you don't find God's Master Plan for your life and start moving forward in it, you just might live with anxiety, live in fear, and be depressed and upset that everyone you know seems to be moving ahead in life while you are in the same place.

November 20
As we move into the age of new "knowledge and revelation" we must come to the place that we realize life is now too big for us to handle by ourselves. We must move beyond our physical and reach into the spiritual where God Himself is: this is a place where there is unlimited help, possibilities, and resources.

November 21
Today, make a decision to believe everything God has promised to do for and through you, instead of believing what you see, hear or feel.

November 22
There will be times you will not feel God's presence or His love. These are the times you have to believe and know that God is there, loving you unconditionally. If you don't, your mind will bring about all kinds of negative and damaging thoughts, putting pressure on you to stop believing God loves you. Just because you feel "spiritually dried-up" doesn't change a thing. God said He would never leave us, nor forsake us. Keep believing, keep trusting, keep the faith.

November 23
Although you may not realize it, many of you cultivated deep spiritual roots while growing up. You may have felt like the odd person at school, or you were insecure, or you experienced constant loneliness. Despite those feelings, you always knew how to connect people with other people, bringing them together for various reasons. You had the ability to inspire people who were down and despondent with feelings of hopelessness and helplessness. Today, I pray and urge you to come forth in your purpose on this earth. You bring healing, strength, and hope to a world that has been waiting for your arrival. You were born for such a time as this!

NOVEMBER 24

This week, consider becoming part of or starting a community that will look individuals in their eyes with unconditional and unspeakable love, allowing them to experience great peace. Your very presence will be God's prescription for angry, depressed, hurting, lonely, and upset individuals.

NOVEMBER 25

Today, take a few minutes to bless and pray for America and other countries and nations of the world. When we pray and speak God's blessings over people, circumstances, and situations, this sends forth the Spirit of God to do just that!

NOVEMBER 26

Whether it's a weekday, weekend, or holiday, it's still important for you to keep your daily communion with God. This should always be your number one priority, especially during the weekend and holidays. Don't allow the busyness of life to draw you from your daily fellowship with God. There are answers you need to receive from Him on weekends and holidays, too. Inspire your children with this priority!

NOVEMBER 27

Our lives will be changed and empowered, all would be well in both our life and our soul, and we would be a mighty force for God in bringing healing to the world IF we make time to be still, commune, and listen to the whispers of God.

NOVEMBER 28

When you are empowered by God, you know that God is your Source, Provision, and Protection. You don't complain and murmur about anything. You stand and face challenges head on, knowing that God has all answers to every situation that comes your way. When you are not empowered by God, you will complain and grumble about many things (if not all things).

NOVEMBER 29

Today, live in full assurance and confidence that God loves you!

NOVEMBER 30

When your energy, focus, intentions, and thoughts are on keeping bad things away from happening to you, you are in reality bringing bad things into your life. Why? Because this is where your awareness lives. If you change your awareness on receiving good things to happen in your life, this is what will happen.

December 1
Today, take time to "intentionally" look for positive things in yourself and in others. I know you will find more than you could ever imagine.

December 2
Whatever inner image you have of yourself will always match your outer self. To change the outer self, including your associations and connections, you will have to spend time in prayer and meditation. It will not happen overnight, especially if the images you want to change have been there for years. But it can be done. Ask God for help. Let the change begin today!

December 3
The moment we stop complaining and worrying about situations in our life will be the moment God can send forth His angels to start working on our behalf. We tie the hands of God when we look at the challenges of life through our physical eyes. All of our problems can be solved with a spiritual solution if only we would believe.

December 4
If your life is so busy because the things you do take so much of your time to maintain—leaving you very little or no time to meditate, pray, and spend quality time with God—you need to simply your life as soon as possible! There should never be anything more important than spending time with and in the presence of God!

DECEMBER 5

Your readiness to change is an important part of your ability to achieve the dreams God has placed in your life!

DECEMBER 6

When you begin to see things as God sees them, you only see possibilities. Every day is beautiful. Every day is wonderful. Every day is filled with sunshine.

DECEMBER 7

Many times we cannot see the wonderful things going on and working in our lives because we are too busy looking at things that are not working in our lives. Once you open your eyes to the possibilities of the great and wonderful things that are in your life, then the light of God shines upon your soul.

DECEMBER 8

It will take courage to move into the things God is calling you to do. Each day will bring opportunities that will challenge your faith. Don't give in or give up. Continue to trust God as your source, your provision, and your protection. As you do, the challenges will eventually become under your feet with you walking above them.

DECEMBER 9

Complaining will add weakness to your life. If you want to live in the blessings of God, the complaining stops. Or you can live in darkness and complain about life and it's challenges. You can't live in both places at the same time. Something to consider today.

December 10

Over the next few days, find reasons to be happy! Make a decision that you are going to be happy one way or another—no matter what. If you have to ignore people, you are going to be happy. If you don't see your boyfriend or girlfriend, you are going to be happy. If you see the person that did you wrong, you will find something about that person that will make you happy. Even if you have a physical handicap, you are going to be happy.

December 11

When we look back at our past and feel condemnation, we lose connection with God. God only looks at our future.

December 12

As we reach and seek for things of God, we open the doors to receive blessings, both spiritually and naturally (in the physical realm). The response becomes effortless from God, because now we are at the place that we desire and want positive change in our lives.

December 13

I'm not sure if there is such a thing as "perfect timing" when it comes to stepping out in faith to the things God has called you to do. If the Spirit says, "Now is the time," then you need to move into those things, no matter how challenging, demanding, or unfriendly the circumstances seem.

December 14

Today, regardless of the challenges you are facing, take time to connect with God, and then find someone to inspire.

December 15

Don't have the attitude that you are above doing things that might seem unexciting, dull, or a waste of your time as you journey through life. Although it may not be something you delight in doing, if you don't pick up that piece of trash left on the floor in the restroom by someone else when directed by God to do so, you are showing God you can't be trusted to obey the effortless things when asked. How can you succeed in the difficult things God will place on your heart and in your path later on down the road?

December 16

Many will wait for a crisis to occur in their lives before starting a daily prayer and meditation time. They will soon realize they are not strong enough in spiritual things as they should be to handle them. There is no such thing as an overnight success when it comes to things of the Spirit. You will have to spend time being still, being present, cultivating a relationship with God, not just when you feel like it but on a persistent basis. Then, when a crisis appears, you will have spiritual solutions.

December 17

When you become conscious of the fact that you are attached and connected to the Source, you will realize all your desires and needs are already taken care of. You will then reach and receive with your faith from the Source those things in in the invisible world, and you will bring those things into your visible world.

December 18

Life with God can be such an adventure and as simply as taking the trash out to the Dumpster. Those few minutes of following God's lead can change a person's life more than they could ever imagine.

December 19

I want to encourage you today. You are not strange, weird, or abnormal. You are perfect in the eyes of God. You are such a contributor to the world, changing and touching lives in so many ways! Take time to meditate and pray for divine relationships to come into your life. There are individuals who are very similar to you and that can relate to you: those with an almost identical outlook on life. They are waiting to meet you, too!

December 20

Here is an opportunity for you to consider before heading to bed: communicate to three people via phone call, e-mail, text message, etc. that you "love them and are praying blessings over their life." Something this simple will make a world of difference in their lives tonight (yours, too)!

DECEMBER 21
Once we align our desires up with the desires of God, we will receive knowledge and wisdom from God that will flow through us; it's the wisdom that created the worlds, the stars, all living things, seen and unseen. Then comes our true destiny, passion, and faith, knowing all things are possible, moving from a "belief" consciousness to a "knowing" consciousness.

DECEMBER 22
When God puts a desire in your soul to do something new, something you have not done before, it becomes your choice to move in that direction. When you move forward, you will find that God has already prepared the way for you to be successful. Yes, God has your back!

DECEMBER 23
Today, make a conscious effort to reject any negative thoughts, negative actions, or negative speech. Let your thoughts, actions, and speech be associated to and connected with being positive, grateful and thankful!

DECEMBER 24
Ask the Spirit to bring individuals into your life who want to get rid of the stony heart they have. They want to receive divine revelation and transformation so they can help others do the same. You are that miracle they are waiting for.

DECEMBER 25

Today, let your desire be to build hope and a family of people who will support and love one another unconditionally. Show them how to take off the mask, put off the show, and let you help them find who they were designed to be. Help them start living a real life that has purpose.

DECEMBER 26

When you start your day off communicating with God, your body will, in time, start cooperating with you: for example, overlooking the tiredness and sleepiness. It will eventually come to the place where it looks forward to the fellowship. After a while, you will never be the same ever again.

DECEMBER 27

Make a decision to not have to be faced with circumstances that will force you to seek the things of the Spirit for answers. Live a life in which the answers are always available, at your fingertips. Make time daily in communion with God. If you do, desperate times will be few and far between.

DECEMBER 28

Do you know that there are individuals who are just as extreme as you when it comes to things of the Spirit? Yes, you are not the only one committed to seeking the Spirit's wisdom for all your problems, walking in unconditional love to everyone you meet and forgiving those that have wronged you at the very first moment the incident happens. You are one of many.

DECEMBER 29

It is possible to live and walk in the love of God in our present time with all people. It will take faith and practice (on purpose) to accomplish this. It will take faith, moving from believing to knowing that there is no failure, only success when we walk in love. The greatest reward from walking this way is that no one is left behind or without!

DECEMBER 30

A new year is approaching and here is a great opportunity to ask God about your mission for the new year. Once you hear from Him, follow His lead, knowing that He has already prepared the way for all things to work according to His purpose for your life.

DECEMBER 31

There will always be opportunities for you to put compassion into action. It's not about feeling sympathy for people but in doing what you are able to do for them. You have the resources to feed the hungry, the power to heal the sick, and you have the love to set them free. My prayer is that you will become so moved as you touch those within your reach with the compassion of God. Thousands are waiting just for you.

CPSIA information can be obtained
at www.ICGtesting.com
Printed in the USA
LVOW10s1549181217
560168LV00035B/2640/P

9 781517 701109